are you the Woman at the Well?

Zella M. Burno

Are You the Woman at the Well? by Zella M. Burno

This book is written to provide information and motivation to readers. Its purpose is not to render any type of psychological, legal, or professional advice of any kind. The content is the sole opinion and expression of the author, and not necessarily that of the publisher.

Copyright © 2020 by Zella M. Burno

All rights reserved. No part of this book may be reproduced, transmitted, or distributed in any form by any means, including, but not limited to, recording, photocopying, or taking screenshots of parts of the book, without prior written permission from the author or the publisher. Brief quotations for noncommercial purposes, such as book reviews, permitted by Fair Use of the U.S. Copyright Law, are allowed without written permissions, as long as such quotations do not cause damage to the book's commercial value.

ISBN: 978-1-952822-93-3 (Paperback)
ISBN: 978-1-952822-92-6 (Digital)

Library of Congress Control Number: 2020923819

Printed in the United States of America.

Dedication

I dedicate my book to my Children. Scherell A. Seldon, Kendall Casey Miller. In memory of my husband Timothy L. Burno [deceased 2011] and my Daughter Dana M. Miller [2012] all my Grandchildren, Theresa J. Miller, Anthony Butler Jr. My Great Grands, Sabriyah Henderson, Dalil Washington, Aria Marie Long. To Mr. and Mrs. Anthony Butler Sr, Pastor Jamie Sanders, First Lady Priscilla Sanders, Elder Evelyn Stephenson and family. To all the members at Virtue Missionary Baptist Church. To Dorothy Burno and family. To all the Carroll, Cone, Donaldson, and Burno families. The Mack Family, The Miller Family.

To my God Daughter Wanshienda Murphy and family] Deacon Herman Reed and Rev. Loretta Reed and family. To my Philadelphia families at The Beulah Baptist Church, Pleasant Grove Baptist Church, People's Baptist Church. Sister United for Christ,

Pastor Altressa Boatwright and family, Apostle Angelia Jeffery and family. Eddie Mae Curry, and Patricia Sapp and family. Tonara Canty and family. Jackie Burrs, Jocelyn and family.

Sister Connection outreach Ministries

To the Miracle Media Press Publishing Company. Sister Earlene Craig and family. To all the Lee Specials and their families with love.

To all Sisters all over the world. Be bless at the Well of Jesus.

8-6-08 Praise Him

Contents

DEDICATION III
ARE YOU THE WOMAN AT THE WELL ? 1
THE REAL PICTURE 9
TRYING TO GET THROUGH THE DAY 11
SIN IS SIN NO MATTER WHAT 19
THANK GOD FOR JESUS 23
WE HAVE A NEED 25
OUR JOB 31
NOW CONSIDER HER MORNING 35
CAN YOU IMAGINE HOW 39
SANCTIFIED WOMAN 47

1

Are you the woman at the well?

This book is about the woman at the well. It tells of her strengths and weaknesses. What women face in daily living? How to face opposition, in trying times. Visualizing yourself as you focus on her condition.

Knowing Jesus can fix it for you when you trust Him.

The woman at the well dwelt with many issues. She had so many hidden agendas. She dwelt with shame, depression, oppression, disgust, and not having a wholesome fellowship with her neighbors. Wondering should she worship God in this mountain or in Jerusalem.

Sin is our background because of the Adamic nature, which causes us to deal with the same problems.

We are all human beings, put in a certain environment we to would be confronted with the same issues.

Thank God, for the second Adam. Who is Jesus himself, our natural nature is polluted with the world of sensuality.

Jesus loves us so much gave us his Divine nature.

His divine nature gives us the power to stop doing worldly things. His power is called resurrected power.

In order to live for Jesus, we must have Jesus nature living inside.

His power takes the desire of sin from your mind and leaves you with the victory of joy. The thought of knowing Jesus loves us so much that He made sure we would have His total being living inside of us in the person of the Holy Spirit.

We need the mind of Christ in us.

Philippians 2:5

We as Christians must let the mind of Christ takes over by receiving the mind of Christ to be in us.

One time we were without hope, until Jesus came and died on the cross for our sin and the whole world.

Realizing that I was a sinner, and needed to be saved, I except Him as my personal Saviour.

Thank God for the blood of Jesus Christ is still able to save souls. The Blood is still alive, still possesses the power to cleanse us from all our sins. 1st John 1:9

We must take our sin problem to Jesus. He has the power to handle it if we ask Him. Jesus is the bridge to get us to Heaven.

He knew we could not get there with our sinful nature. He gave us His divine nature. His nature, we can receive all the heavenly blessings. And enjoy peace, love, and rest, in our spirit and soul.

> Blessed be the God and Father of our Lord Jesus Christ, who hath blessed us with all spiritual blessings in heavenly places in Christ.
>
> Eph. 1:3

> For God so loved the world that he gave his only begotten son that who so ever believeth in him shall not perish but have everlasting life.
>
> John 3:16

The requirement is to believe on the Lord Jesus Christ and be saved.

I thank God, every day for loving me, and loving the people of the world. The lord made it possible forever body to accept His Son Jesus So they could live in heaven when death comes. The door is open for us all. The choice is ours to make.

God gave us free will. We have the choice of who we are going to serve.

We can serve the lord Jesus Christ or the Devil.

The choice is ours to make. God loves people but hates their sins.

What will keep you from going to heaven?

By not excepting, His Son Jesus Christ as your personal Saviour. We send ourselves to hell. But God the Father had a plan.

Jesus said to prepare me a body I will go down and save mankind.

> Then said I, Lo, I come in the volume of the book it is written of me.
>
> I delight to do thy will, O my God: yea, thy law is written in my heart.
>
> Psalm 40:7,8

And she shall bring forth a son and thou shall call his name Jesus: for he shall his people from their sins.

St. Matthew 1:21

Jesus had a prepared body to do His Father's will. The Father so loved us so much that He gave His only begotten Son. Jesus steps up to the plate and hit a home run. By dying, on the Cross for our sins. Thank you, Jesus.

No matter what our past consists of. No one should really look down their nose at anybody. We all need Jesus.

Jesus did not discriminate at all. He uses whores, prostitutes, drunks, gamblers, murders, etc. to work in His kingdom. And such were some of you. Thank God, we were washed in the blood of the lamb. Praise the Lord for his goodness.

We all need to go to the well for salvation. At the well of Salvation, you will find joy to help you to endure this journey.

Every person need to meet Jesus at the well. Our natural man gets thirsty on the journey. Our spiritual being gets thirsty also. Only Jesus knows how to quench our hungry and thirsty.

We have a body a soul, and a spirit. What you may call a trichotomy. The body is the material part of man that houses the soul and makes him earth conscious.

The soul is that immaterial part of man that makes him self-conscious and enables him to express himself.

The soul is the seat of the appetites, the desires, and the will.

The soul has reasoned imaginations, memory, and confidence.

The emotional part of the soul is sorrow, joy, love, fear, etc.

The spirit is that immaterial part of man that makes him God-conscious and able to know and fellowship with -God.

The spiritual man can worship God. [John4:24]

The spiritual man can have peace. [Isa. 26:3, Rom.5:1, Phil. 4:7]

The word will wash and cleanse you.

Your soul and spirit are dealt with through the word.

> For the word of God is quick, and powerful, and sharper than any two-edged sword, piercing even to the dividing asunder of soul and spirit, and of the joints and marrow, and is a discerner of thoughts and intents of the heart.
>
> Hebrews 4:12.

He knew us before the foundation of this world. `

> Be not thou therefore ashamed of the testimony of our Lord, nor of me his prisoner: but be thou partaker of the afflictions of the gospel according to the power of God: Who hath saved us, and called us with a holy calling, not according to our works, but according to his own purpose and grace, which was given in Christ Jesus before the world began
>
> 2 Timothy 1:8,9

There was a call on the woman in a good life. Before the foundation of the world, God had an eternal purpose for her life. She had no idea when she arrived at the well that it was her season. She walked into her season. Jesus was sitting on the well knowing she would be free today.

Jesus dealt with the whole person.

Jesus will meet you at the well.

Your well may be in the bedroom or your car, in the kitchen, is on your knees praying. Where ever there is a need Jesus will go out of the way to meet you.

The Samaritan woman was in trouble, with heavy loads on her shoulder. Jesus went out of his way to go through Samaria.

> And he must need to go through Samaria.
>
> John 4:4

When you look at this, the verse you can see Jesus had a divine must in his spirit. By him being all knowing God, The Omnipotent God.

Who has all power in his hand?

He knew that this woman needed deliverance from sin. He also knew she would be the right candidate for the job of witnessing in her community. It was not based on what she did it was based on who Jesus is.

> And she shall bring forth a son, and thou shall call his name Jesus: for he shall save his from their sins.
>
> St. Matthews 1:21

When Jesus showed up that was her season.

The almighty purpose work is in Eternity now.

When the time of the season is fully come Jesus will show up and show out. For his divine purpose, must be fulfilled.

Just like God had an eternal purpose for Jesus

> According to the eternal purpose which he purposed in Christ Jesus our Lord.
>
> Eph.3:11

Before the foundation of the world, he knew that this time would be for the woman at the well. There are no surprises with our God. Keep the faith He will sit on your wall.

The Omniscience God, who knows all things. He knew she needed some living water. She needed a change in her life. We also need a change in our life. When we get stuck in a relationship and do not know which way to go. Our friends cannot help us, because they have burdens

But Jesus has the power to bring us out to perfect praise of thanksgiving. We must have a need to know him, and to desire to love on him with all of our might.

We need an intimate relationship with Jesus. What a fellowship What a joy divine, leaning on his everlasting arm. A real need will make you seek Jesus. You would find yourself losing the desire of the world because your heart wants Jesus to meet your needs.

> Let us therefore come boldly unto the throne of grace that we may obtain mercy, and find grace to help in time of need.
>
> Hebrews 4:16

A need will summon grace to your situation. A need will increase your faith to believe God. A need will may your prayer life longer in the presence of God. God's amazing grace will bring a change in your mind and in your heart.

The word must in The New Strong's Complete Dictionary of Bible Words. States that it was necessary [dei][opheilo] to owe; to be under obligation. To behoove, be bound, be debt, be due, be guilty [indebted][must] needs ought to owe, should. With these definitions I can see the due change in her life, and in my life. I must keep Jesus in my life because he is my life.

I like the thought that Jesus was bound to set her free. He meets all of her needs. Only he has the power to do this.

> But my God shall supply all your need according to his riches in glory by Christ Jesus.
>
> Phil. 4:19

Know [perceive, recognize, and understand with approval] that the Lord is God! It is He who has made us, not we ourselves [and we are His]! We are His people and the sheep of His pasture.

Psalms 100:3 Amplified Bible

For we are God's [own] handiwork [His workmanship], recreated in Christ Jesus. [Born anew] that we may do those good works which God predestined [planned beforehand] for us [taking paths which He prepared ahead of time], that we should walk in them [living the good life which He prearranged and made ready for us to live].

Eph. 2:10

I am so glad I belong to Jesus.

2

The real picture

When you look at the real picture of what was happening at that time you will understand the must needs to go through Samaria. At the time Jesus was just beginning his ministry.

There were problems between the Jews and the Samaritans. The Jews did ever thing they could not pass through Samaria. Jesus took the short cut and went through Samaria From Judea to Galilee meant passing through a central territory called Samaria. If he has to reach way down He will pick you up. The Samaritan woman was indebted to sin. Her lifestyle was obnoxious to the community.

Having had five husbands of course the community would wonder about her. What we do in the past will confront you in the future. Keep living you will see it again.

But do not let the past eat up your future. We must forget about it, and give it over to Jesus with his blood he can purge our conscience clean. He is the only one who can take the pain out of your past. He would give you joy like a river that flows out of your being.

Our conscience must be purged. [Hebrews 9:14] His Blood has to purge out all our old self-thoughts, from birth to the day you accept Jesus as your personal savior.

All those thoughts must be purged. Once the cleansing, then you can serve the living God, in spirit and truth. The blood cleanses our inner man, [which is the heart] so that the Holy Spirit can dwell in our being. The blood has never lost its power. The Holy Spirit does not live in an unclean temple.

Looking back in history [this is coming out of The Life Application Bible] After the Northern Kingdom, with its capital at Samaria, fell to the Assyrians, many Jews were deported to Assyria. And foreigners were brought in to settle the land and keep the peace.

[2 Kings 17:24]. The intermarriage between those foreigners and the remaining Jews resulted in a mixed race, impure in the opinion of Jews who lived in the Southern Kingdom.

Thus the pure Jews hated the mixed-race, called Samaritans. Because they felt that their fellow Jews who had intermarried had betrayed their people and nation.

The Samaritans had set up an alternate center for worship on Mount Gerizim [4:20] to parallel the Temple at Jerusalem, but it had been destroyed 150 years earlier.

While there was long-standing prejudice between Jews and Samaritans, Jesus did not live by such restrictions. The route through Samaria was shorter, and that was the route he took.

Jacob's well was on the property originally owned by Jacob [Genesis 33:18,19]. It was not a spring-fed well, but a well into which water seeped from rain and dew, collecting at the bottom. Wells was always located outside the city along the main road.

3

Trying to get through the day

Twice each day, morning and evening, women came to draw water. This woman came at noon, however, to avoid meeting people who knew her reputation. You know how we do not want to speak to anybody, we will go another way. But God still sees us. He knows the true heart of the matter.

Let us consider her morning when she awoke. Thinking how will she get through the day, with her needs being so on fire? Lust has a way of taking us to some places we really had no plan to go. Because of ignorance, not understanding the real consequences.

Sometimes our self-esteem can get so low that we really do not feel like living. The enemy will attack your mind so severely. You must fight to stay above the water. Water could be a type of trouble.

Her mind was consumed with so many voices and problems attacking her at one time. Being in trouble will keep you in fellowship with Jesus, you have to turn lemons into lemonade. How sweet it is in Jesus. There are some hurts that you cannot explain. They are so deeply rooted in our spirit until it causes you to fake it until you make it.

Most of the time our smile is not real, because our inside is so bound up with years of unforgiveness, angry, jealousy, hatred and bitterness. Some of us are still carrying hurts from our childhood. With all these spirits holding you hostage in your everyday walk, leaving you sad with the camouflage of joy. Sisters, we need a drink of Jesus' living waters.

Jesus gave this woman an extraordinary message about fresh and pure water that would quench her thirst forever.

The Samaritan woman was a woman of the hated mixed race. She was known for living in sin. The well was a public place that she visited only at noontime when no one else was around. Jesus knew her thoughts as well as her sin-sick condition. He had a need for this Samaritan woman. He can use anybody from every walk of life. You cannot get to dirty for Jesus. He saves drunkards, liars, whoremongers, gamblers,

Every human being was born with a sinful nature.

> For all have sinned, and come short of the glory of God.
>
> Romans 3:23

Jesus is the only one who can take us out of the devil's hands.

It is a spiritual battle. We must have a new nature. The old nature is corrupt and sinful; with our new divine nature we can now trust the Holy Ghost to lead us into all truth.

Our new nature is spiritual, which allows us to communicate with the Father

At the Cross is where He conquered the devil.

> [The Father] has delivered and drawn us to Himself out of the control and the dominion of darkness and has transferred us into the kingdom of the Son of His love. In whom we have our redemption through His blood, [which means] the forgiveness of our sins. [Now] He is the exact the likeness of the unseen God [the visible representation of the invisible]; He is the firstborn of all creation. For it was in Him that all things were created, in heaven and on earth. Things are seen and unseen, whether thrones, dominion, rulers, or authorities; all things were created and exist through Him [by His service, intervention] and in for Him. And He Himself existed before all things, and in Him all things consist [cohere, are held together].
>
> Colossians 2:13 – 17] Amplified
Prov. 8:22-31

The battle was totally the Lord's battle. The best witness is the ones who have been there and done that. Her social statics was well rounded in dark places. By Jesus being the light of the world, He can light up her darkness, and send her out as a beaming light to do his will.

> For thou wilt light my candle: the LORD my God will enlighten my darkness.
>
> Psalm 18:28

How many times has Jesus shone his light into your darkness?

The dark place, where you could not share with anyone. Sometimes so burdened, which make you stay to yourself and cry. Hoping, no one could detect that you are in pain.

Crying on the inside and trying to fake it on the outside. One of the worst hurt we women encounter is to find out our mate is cheating on us. The trust factor breaks down in our minds. Jealousness starts standing up in our minds. Every time our mate talks to someone we become furious. We get upset when our love is taken for granted. A lot of time we are treated like dogs. The outside woman is treated like a queen.

Thank God, we can run to Jesus. He sooth our heart and calm our fears. He gives us comfort that draws us closer to Him. Jesus knows how to treat us with tender loving care. He is always caring for us. The power of the Holy Ghost who has the mind of God gives us comfort and joy.

I can stand up on His word. I can trust His word; Jesus went to the Cross to prove He loves me. So many women are in the church because they love and the way Jesus talks. He always has a word for us ladies. He gives us wisdom on how to take care of our homes. Jesus is a loving man.

Yes, I look at how many times Jesus had to deliver me from darkness and translate me into the kingdom of his living Son. Nobody could help me but Jesus. There is a place in my house call knee valley. Troubles will make you drop down in the knee valley for help and guidance.

When you view trouble, you will find out that trouble will teach you how to seek God. David said.

> Though I walk in the midst of trouble, thou wilt revive me: thou shalt stretch forth thine hand against the wrath of mine enemies and thy right hand shall save me.
>
> Psalm 138:7,8

There is a revival that comes out of trouble. Trouble will make you Godly conscious. It will cause your flesh to die. All that trouble won't kill out; God's consuming fire will do the rest. Trouble has a way of making you lose your grip.

It seems like your eyes get clearer and sharper. You are so thankful to the Father for delivering you; you do not have time to judge anyone. Oh, by the grace of God there goes me.

Let us really look at this woman's situation. She was hurting very badly on the inside. She had lost five husbands. The bible does not say whether they were divorced or died. Never the less she had to be strong to stand up under her misfortune of losing her 5 husbands.

The depression of going through these five ordeals is a beautiful picture of a strong woman. When I look at her situation you could see that she needed supper natural strength and some living water from the master.

When I think of what I have experienced being married three times. I can understand the strength of this woman. My first marriage was very abusive. Dealing with alcohol, women, and a whole lot of cursing.

Ladies this is abuse. Do not take it likely, because it is going to get worse. My second one died, after divorcing him. He was abusive too. I waited 22 years before I got married again. This was a God-sent man. Jesus met me at the well. I can see a strong woman with a strong will to make it through this life. Women we are so amazing to multitask through our problems, and still have joy in the midst of crying. [Thank you, Jesus]

Having five husbands in a period of time will cause any woman to be cautious on every hand. The Bible said the six-man were not hers as being married to him. Just a situation in her heart. Hurt behind losing five husbands.

She did not trust herself to be married again. Long as she had a man in her life. Some women; are like that today. Rather than to be alone, some would work and take care of a man just to say I got a man.

Do you really have a man? Or does the man have you? Just having someone to be in the house with you, does not mean he is your man. His life is still an option. Until he put a ring on your finger and say I do in marriage. He is not your man. Just someone you are taking care of every day. The sad thing about it, he belongs to so many other women besides you. Clean your house and run to the well where Jesus is.

We do not see Jesus until trouble comes into our hearts. The pain of trouble will be a teacher for life. Pain has a way of awaking us up to the truth. It is what it is. Now we have to deal with it. Some time we are addicted to pain. [Just doing dumb things] We as women need someone who will love us unconditionally no matter what our circumstances are. A little hurt will not kill you, it will make you have boldness down in your gut to stand your ground. Do not let your flesh overtake you.

It is the thought of feeling good, I cannot get enough of sex. You feel like the man is your god. Being obsessed with your flesh only leads to more darkness. Even willing to fight out of character over a loose man. We can be so messed up. Looking, for love in the wrong places. I can relate to this woman at the well. Her strong qualities are outstanding in my mind. The condition she lived in with all her problems, she still could be used by the master. But she had to be cleaned up first. Jesus knows who we are, and he understands our hurts and bruises in this life. He knows all about the innermost depths of our wants, needs, and satisfaction.

He made us, so he knows what is best for us. A lot of time it is not the flesh that needs to be satisfied the way we think, our spirit man has a thirst and a hunger for the true living God. Our spirit can be so deprived of peace, joy, and love until it feels like the flesh is on fire.

> As the hart panteth after the water brooks, so panteth my soul after thee, O God. My soul thirsteth for God, for the living God; when shall I come and appear before God.
>
> Psalms 42:1, 2

Trouble can bring you to the well of life. There you meet Jesus one on one. You do not care who sees you or who hears you all you want is a relief.

Only Jesus can really heal our hearts from the strong callous of hurt. I wonder to my self, could I have held up like this woman at the well. Yes I can see my self in this picture in many ways.

Divorce sometimes is worst than death. Because in death it is final, but with a divorce, you still see you're hurt. When I look back I know I was glad when Jesus came to me, he met me on my knees crying out to be saved from playing numbers. Gambling is just as bad as adultery. Hurt from an abusive marriage. Knowing that you have to raise three children by yourself. It is not easy to raise children by yourself. You become overwhelmed. Your nerves stay fired up. No one sees that you need some help. All they can see you doing a good job raising the children.

When your body is crying for some relief. Your mind is hanging on a thread trying to think. Only Jesus can really give you that relief. He knows your heart and your spirit and your mind. Lord, you know how to deliver me. Call upon the Lord while He is near. He will deliver you and keep you in the midst of your troubles.

And every time you see the ex-husband you wish he was still yours. Then you start asking your self should I have done this or that, maybe we could have made it. Even in all the pain at that time, the fear of being alone raises its head. Only the power of prayer brings us through our misfortune. There is a loneliness that you encounter when you get a divorce. You may have the paper but your mind and your being are all out of the sink. You think about all the years you have a loss and you cannot get them back. Now you have to struggle through the unknown to get yourself back on track. The battle of your mind is at stake. You have to feed your spirit with the word of God so you can keep a sound mind to live on without your mate.

4

Sin is sin no matter what

I live in an abusive marriage for 13 years. I had 3 children. My husband at that time drank and ran the streets. We had no food at times. And very few cloths. But I was still smiling like everything was alright.

Dumb and afraid and still feeling love for him is a very heavy load in your heart. I dealt with what was happening to me. I prayed and stayed in Church with my children. A lot of time I hated to go home.

A lot of shame and depression. The hurting thing was when he would bring home some whiskey and not food. He would buy himself a walking suit so he could look good. I needed stocking and could not even buy some. I kept my home clean, in spite of the hell I was encountering. My children were clean. I did without for my children's sake. I put them first. We had to make it the best way we could. A mother's job is to protect her children. When I did go to the store to buy some food, he would not get up off his but to bring the food up the stairs. We live on the 2nd floor. I can relate to troubles and your husband staying out for three and four days. I was blessed to meet Jesus at the well one day.

Jesus filled me with his living waters. Yes, I can relate in many ways with her inner self. Being a shamed about the things you have to do. To survive, through the day, Feeling empty inside. Crying on the inside, but forcing a smile of joy in the presence of your peers.

Yes, it does hurt deep down inside. You cannot tell people what you are really going through at the time of the pain. All you know is that your world has changed, and you have to trust the lord to guide you through the dark valley of despair.

It takes all you have to get up and face the daybreak. Wondering how you are going to take care of your family and still smile and be happy. We as women are good actresses. Things we covered up and pretend to be happy at. Even though the time was different, men are still men. And women are still women. She needed some relief. A walking time bomb, of pain and hurt.

Jesus was the only one who really could see her for what it was worth to her. He loves us so much no distance could be in the way. He had a mandate that was mandatory to see the woman free at the well.

Jesus saw both sides of her. The flesh side and the spiritual side of her. Just like he sees both sides of us. The inside and the outside.

> Neither is there any creature that is not manifest in his sight: but all things are naked and opened unto the eyes of him with whom we have to do.
>
> Heb. 4:13

God sees everything. There is no darkness in him at all. What a mighty God we serve. Jesus saw that her spirit was in darkness. He knew she needed a change in her life. The pain she was carrying from all six men. We woman always chew on what we have experienced. Yes we need to share with others, so they can get delivered.

Just to hear Jesus' voice penetrated her whole being. Her spirit started to come alive. Her mind was shaken up because she never heard a man talk to her like that. HIS voice melted her soul. She wanted to know more about Jesus. Never a man spoke that kind and sweet to her. She was mesmerized by the Savior Jesus Christ Himself. His words filled her heart with love. The power of Jesus' words snatched her from the darkness that had lived so long in her mind. His words quicken her spirit with love and joy. We as women love a man that speaks kind words to us. Especially, when he takes time to listen to us.

In the 7th verse Jesus saith to her give me a drink. She brought up the fact that Jews hath no dealings with the Samaritans. Now this is when it gets interesting.

[v.10] Jesus answered and said unto her, If thou knewest the gift of God, and who it is that saith to thee, give me to drink; thou wouldest have asked of him, and he would have given thee living water. One thing about us women we are very curios when a man says he is going to give us something. A lot of us cannot wait. Jesus, being Jesus talks to the Samaritan Woman with respect and with love. These are some of the things she was missing. What a sweet voice our Saviour has.

Meeting him at the well was her blessing. She needed some relief from pain. She could see that another marriage was not the answer to her problem. She needed spiritual help. Her spirit needed to be lifted passes her flesh. Because your flesh can cause you to be kept in darkness, with no hope in sight. The flesh can cause you to lose all your dignity. Always trying to capture. That first sensation. So you start chasing what you felt was the ultimate good feeling. He knows why we go astray. We have a sensitive make up. His well is always open for us to drink. He knew we would get thirsty one day. Just like he had a must need to go through Samaria, he also has a must need to take care of us.

She was rejected in her community by the women. Because of her lifestyle of living they were saying some ugly things about her. Some women can be very picky. The hair, the clothes, the house, and the car. Just think about how we made it through the day, sometimes we did not feel like getting up. Very depressed, no money, bills not paid, and my children's father did not want to work. In spite of what was going on, I still kept a clean home for my family.

He was very abusive to me and the children. Always cursing at everything, having his whiskey with no food in the house. Pregnant with a child, and a 3-year-old looking to me, for something to eat. Yes, I can relate. I needed Jesus to meet me at the well.

What a picture. But I needed a well for Jesus to meet me. I called on Jesus for help, and he delivered me. Save me from all of my depression and gave me light and knowledge to walk out of abusive marriage.

You cannot leave an abusive marriage on your own. You have to trust God to deliver you from evil. He is the only one who knows everything.

He will shine the light for you to run to safety, just trust him.

5

Thank God for Jesus

Thank God for Jesus loving us so much that he will bless us in spite of social conditions. There is no situation that can keep Jesus out. Even sin has to bow to the blood because the blood of Jesus washes away all sin.

> If we confess our sins, he is faithful and just to forgive us our sins, and to cleanse us from all unrighteousness. If we say that we have not sinned, we make him a liar, and his word is not in us.
>
> 1 John 1:9-10

Our responsibility is to confess our sins, whether they are large or small. Do not let your mind override the word of God. The word is true. Our natural minds are corrupt. This is why we need the mind of Christ, so we can operate spiritually. We must operate out of a renewed mind.

> A carnal mind is an enemy to God
>
> Romans 8:7-10

We all have a must need for Jesus in our life.

Now that we understand the background of this must need to go through Samaria. We do have a Samaria in our lives. Some folks hate us, they are unsociable to us. many times we find ourselves in a dark valley of despair. Seeking help in the wrong places, looking for love from the wrong source. Putting our trust in men, instead of trusting Jesus. So many times we trust the wrong men. They are not working, they want to sleep around, they find excuses why they do not work. Many times we make them our baby sitters without really understanding, that men do not want to baby sit. When the natural father does not want to babysit, what makes you think the boyfriend wants to do it?

Later on, we read in the newspaper that the child has been abused by the boyfriend. Wake up and smell the coffee sister. Take care of your own children. Protect them from harm. A real man of worth will let you stay home. While he goes to work.

> Question:
>> Do you have a must need situation?
>> Because if you do Jesus will meet your needs.

Women, He made us soft so we could huge our families. He gave us a mind to know how to help our husband. He gave us sensitiveness to know what is going on in our families. It is like a 6 sense.

6

We have a need

We all have a need for Jesus many times we get thirsty in our spirit. The pure water that Jesus gives us keeps bubbling up in our well. We have a well that Jesus gave us, and he keeps us filled with his pure water. Then he touches our bellies so that we can release the living waters to others. We have to believe and receive so that we can be good vessels. We are his workmanship in Christ Jesus.

> We are anointed to do his will. You must have the blessing of his anointing on you and in you.
>
> Eph. 2:10

> In the last day, that great day of the feast, Jesus stood and cried, saying, if any man thirst, let him come unto me

and drink. He that believeth on me, as the scripture hath said, out of his belly shall flow rivers of living water.

John 7:37, 38

We cannot do anything until we drink from his fountain. The hymn writer wrote there is a fountain filled with blood drawn from Emmanuel vein, where sinners plunge beneath the flood, Lose all their guilty stain. We women love to plunge into good things. Jesus always has good things to plunge into. Let us plunge into his love, his joy, his grace, his favor, his righteousness. His fountain never runs dry. True love brings joy, and joy gives us strength so we can run in the power of his might. This water is so contagious until doubt cannot stop you, discouragement cannot disappoint you. What a mighty God we serve. The woman at the well had for the first time a true foundation. Love is the true foundation of God. Peace works from love, joy works from love, faith works from love. Love knits everything together.

If we do not feed ourselves with the word of God we will be weak and blind to the things of God. Our bellies will be empty, and we cannot do God's work being empty.

This is why so many saints cannot be used by God. Because they have not studied to show themselves approved unto God. God does not work apart from himself. The word is Jesus. We must get him down on the inside of our being. This is done by studying the word of God. So he can live in us and be our life.

> Now, look at this the word is Jesus, and Jesus is the living word. He transforms himself into the written word so we can be filled with the fullness of him. What a mighty God

we serve. We have heavenly transformers living inside of us. [Those that are saved].

Col. 3:3-4

The living word died on the cross, and gave us his Spirit to guide us, so when we read the written word the Holy Spirit breathes in us and shines the light in our spirit so our eyes would be enlightening to see in the spirit realm, and we receive it by faith. Then our soul rejoices in the lord.

Only The Holy Spirit will lead and guide us into all truth. He operates through the word. The Blood operates with the Holy Spirit and they all agree here on earth as one. [1st John 5:8]

Now look at the Amplified Version

> Now on the final and most an important day of the feast, Jesus stood, and He cried in a loud voice if any man is thirsty, let him come to me and drink. He who believes in me [who cleaves to and trusts in and relies on me] as the Scripture has said, from his innermost being shall flow [continuously] springs and rivers of living water.
>
> John 7:37,38

The blessing is that we have a well that springs up in our spirit, with rivers of living water, which flows in our innermost being. Knowing how to keep our well filled is a vital part of Christian living. We have to stay in his word. To keep our spirit-filled we must spend time in prayer. Let the praises of the Lord be lifted up at all times.

> I will bless the Lord at all times. His praises will continually be in my mouth.
>
> Ps. 34:1

Singing, with joy down in our innermost soul. Drawing, from the wells of our salvation. [Isa.12:3-4}

We prime a natural well to receive water so in the spirit realm we prime with singing. With praising him all day long because the joy of the Lord is our strength. [Neh. 8:10b]

In the book of Eph.1:23, we learn that we are his body, the fullness of him that filleth all in all. Jesus must keep his body fill with himself. The more we read and study, the more we are filled with the fullness of the lord. God's love has no shame it covers a multitude of sins.

The woman at the well thought that receiving this living water from Jesus, she would be able to escape her confrontations. Jesus comes to empower us to stand against the wiles of our enemies. To change us from the inside out so we can deal with problems from God's perspective. when we are living wrong, and in sin, we feel unworthy of the true things of God. Looking for acceptance from the wrong people. So many times we pour out our souls to the wrong persons. Looking for God's results from man's flesh.

Being so mixed up in the mind and having a dark spirit, sin will lock you into darkness and ignorance until you are so ashamed of yourself. Now you have to deal with low self-esteem. This makes you feel like you are not good enough. And the first thing we attack is our hair.

The things we do to our head. Some of us women are so lazy about how our appearance looks it is a shame. And you wonder why nobody is looking your way. Please fix yourself up. Keep your children clean, clean your own house. Use the money that you spend on your hot self to buy the cleaning products. Stop being so selfish.

Learn how to cook some food that would stretch for 2days. The money that you spend on fast food could be used to buy some real groceries.

Thank God for real true sisters. They care about us, they can see because of where they have been delivered from in their lifetime. I had a sister when I got depressed and I could not get up to dress myself.

She calls me and curses me out. I got angry and jump up out of the bed, So I could tell her off. She loves me that much to reach me. No matter what she had to use. We laugh about it today. The main thing was to break depression. We must have some true sisters in our life. Some big momma's, and some grand ma's, somebody who will tell the truth.

7

Our job

Our job is to seek him, and wait at the well for him, this well could be when we read our bible, meditate in the word, making melody to him by singing, and praising his name.

> And to know the love of Christ, which passeth knowledge, that ye might be filled with all the fullness of God.
>
> Eph. 3:19

We must be filled with the fullness of God to work for him in the kingdom. We should be focusing on kingdom living.

The Samaritan woman had the living Jesus to give her the living water. We have the risen Christ who gives the living water through the Holy Spirit who gives us revelation knowledge as we study the word.

Then the Holy Spirit reveals to us the living well in our hearts. The living water flows from our heart to our bellies. Because our bellies are filled with what our mouth speaks.

> A man's belly shall be satisfied with the fruit of his mouth, and with the increase of his lips shall he is filled.
> [21]Death and life are in the power of the tongue: and they that love it shall eat the fruit thereof.
>
> Proverbs 18:20, 21

This is why we have to be careful about how we talk about anything. So keep the word of God on your lips and in your mouth. The Holy Spirit will guide you each and every day. We cannot curse at our children and expect them not to curse. Children repeat what they hear. Spend time with your children. Stop letting a man take up all your time. Give some time to your children. This is what is wrong with most of our children. They are looking for love. Hug your children, make them feel that they belong to you. Tell them you love them. Do not buy them. Say a little prayer over your children. Oh, when we talk about the goodness of Jesus our spirit man is leaping for joy.

> Therefore with joy shall ye draw water out of the wells of salvation.
>
> Isaiah 12:3

Jesus is our salvation. Our salvation is in the person of Jesus Christ, and not in the world system.

Our spirit man has to eat the word of God. We need to stay in touch with Jesus. He is the 66 books of the Bible.

The woman at the well met the 66 books at the well. Jesus is our all in all. We can see she had the best deal of her life. Now we have the best deal of our life, the written word.

The seed of life.

> For by him were all things created, that are in heaven, and that are in earth, visible and invisible, whether they be thrones, or dominions, or principalities, or power; all things were created by him, and for him.
>
> Colossians 1:16,17,19

And he is before all things, and by him, all things consist. For it pleased the Father that in him should all fullness dwell Jesus pleased God in all the divine fullness. Before the foundation of the world, he knew that he would meet the woman at the well. It was destined to be so.

8

Now consider her morning

Now consider her morning as she awoke, and wondered how she was going to make it through the day. With her needs so on fire, not having been fully satisfied with what she thought she needed. Her flesh lust-have was taken over her mind wanting to fulfill every moment. She had so many thoughts running through her mind. The flesh does not satisfy. Only Jesus can reach the inner man and deliver us from all its fiery wants. What is going on is deeper than the flesh. This is why we do so many crazy things because we are looking for satisfaction in the flesh. When satisfaction is only in the Lord Jesus Himself.

The man that she now has is not hers. But he was fulfilling her heat in the flesh. Really lusting with no satisfaction. How many times have we women been in some hot relationship with a man which did not mean us any good? Most of the time it was a waste of time. Looking good but could not fulfill anything.

We are just like her. Different times, different places. Her mind had something else to think about besides the man she was living with. She had Jesus on her mind. She knew Jesus was special and different. He did not talk like all the other men that had been in her life.

He was talking about her giving him a drink of water from the well. She knew that she did not have a bucket to draw with. Yet in her mind, she was considering how to give him a drink.

Jesus had captured her mind to give me to drink. You know he does not have to say but one word. Like he said to peter [come] [Matt. 14:28] We women are so curious about what men are thinking, while we are talking to them. Not knowing she was talking to the master himself. Glory. The only good man I know. She began to ask Jesus so many questions about the Jews have no dealings with the Samaritans.

When Jesus does show up in our life, will we recognize him? Or will we be a puzzle at what will be happening to us? Something new has entered our spirit, and we are going to see what this is.

Just like this Samaritan woman. She knew Jesus was different.

> "Then he said unto her If thou knewest the gift of God, and who it is that saith to thee, Give me to drink; thou wouldest have asked of him, and he would have given thee living water".

This is what blew her mind thought. Thinking within herself. What is the gift of God? The thought of someone giving her a gift left her stunned. Now the gift of God is Jesus to the world. St. John 3:16

The gift from Jesus to us is the Holy Spirit. Whatever Jesus had the Samaritan woman wanted it. She told him that she could not draw water because she did not have anything to draw with. Then she said the well is deep: this is from the natural point of view. But she insisted on knowing where Jesus was getting this living water from. Oh when you meet the true Jesus, He will make your brand new, from the inside out. She was no match for Jesus. Even though she recognized that he was greater than their father Jacob. And this is the well where Jesus sat. A spiritual well, sitting on a natural well. The living word speaking into her spirit. All this power operating at Jacob's well. [Praise him]

Jesus knew her whole life and her thoughts.

"He said unto her, who so ever drinketh of this water shall thirst again:"

Natural water is for the natural man. The living water is for the Spiritual Man. The Spiritual Man is not satisfied with natural things.

> "For they that are after the flesh do mind the things of the flesh; but they that are after the Spirit the things of the Spirit."
>
> Rom. 8:5

Jesus had gotten her undivided attention. She was excited in her spirit. This was the first time she could be herself without feeling shame.

While she was talking to Jesus her depression fell off. Her low self-esteem rose up high enough, that she could deal with her situation. Jesus was electrifying to talk too. What a man, what a man. The real man was in town.

"Jesus said to her but who so ever drinketh of the water that I shall give him shall never thirst, but the water that I shall give to him shall be in him a well of water springing up into everlasting life."

She knew this was what she needed in her life. So she said without hesitation, "Sir, give me this water, that I thirst not, neither come hither to draw. Jesus dwelt with her spirit first. He was calling her to be an Evangelist. He empowered her with resurrected power. Even though he was still alive He still was the resurrection.

Jesus said unto her, Go, call thy husband:"

The Prophet in Jesus came forth to work on her. Jesus calls it like it was. He is our Prophet, Priest, and king. The Prophet for tells what is going on in your life.

"The woman answered and said, I have no husband. Jesus said unto her, thou hast well said I have no husband:

Dealing with her life style of sin, can you imagine her feeling lost and guilty? She could not blend in the society of her surroundings because of her reputation. You know how people shun you because of what they said and heard about you. Some you know and, and some you never met. The women of that community must have been very cruel to her.

We know how to mean we can be about another woman at times.

All women are the same as their husbands. The women back then guarding their husband every time she showed up. The men in her life were a little softer toward her.

9

Can you imagine how

Each man brought her a different lifestyle. She had five husbands. Now bear in mind she had five husbands. The Bible does not say whether they died or she was divorced from them.

Five men in your life will bring about change. I will like to deal with some lifestyles that could have been then and is still happening now. Each one had their own style of lovemaking.

As we know sex is never going out of business. This is God's way of reproducing mankind and replenishing the earth. This is why He created marriage. [Genesis 2:21-25] Every husband had a different voice in her spirit. All those voices in her spirit, and her mind while she pondered about her daily living.

Look at us we can just barely handle one man's voice and the children. Even when we try to cheat on our spouse, it just doesn't work. We have to be delivered from all our old lovers. We have to denounce all they were to us. Living for Jesus is meant to be clean and free. Having your conscience purged from all the dead things in your life.[Heb. 9:14] you must have a clean conscience to serve a true and living God. The blood still works. The blood has the power to purge your conscious all the things we have done in our life. It goes down to the very marrow of your bones. The power of the blood will cleanse you from your head to your feet.

> Thou wilt keep him in perfect peace, whose mind is stayed on thee; because of the trusteth in thee.
>
> Isaiah 26:3

[v.4] Trust ye in the LORD forever: for in the LORD JEHOVAH is everlasting strength.

We can take a good lesson from this Samaritan woman. Sometimes we are thinking no one really cares about us the way we are feeling. Who really knew how she felt, and how she needed to be loved. Yet each man had their own agenda while being her husband. Sex does not make you happy, it does make you feel good. True happiness is in Jesus, and Jesus alone.

Notice there is no real happiness in her until she meets Jesus lives. We cannot be happy with love and peace until we meet Jesus. For he is our love and peace.

THE FIVE HUSBANDS

Husband numbered 1

Who look at her through his lustful jealous eyes. I only have eyes for you. Even in marriage, we tend to feel that our husband is more than God at times. We put them on a petal stool and we really worship them. God is our true husband and he is a jealous God over us.

Instead of us looking to God for our source we turn to a man. Looking for God's results from man's flesh. We can be so mixed up in our minds because of our darkness in our spirit. This is why we have to be equally yoked. This way we both can enjoy the things of God. And he gets all the glory.

Even though this was years ago with the woman at the well she was trying to make it with what she had. When you have a jealous husband you are trap in a mindset of what is he going say or do. Being bound by flesh power weakens your whole mindset. Just by hearing the whispering of his voice some time make you nervous.

You be trying to get your story right, so when he started talking about something that does not make any sense you can counteract his thoughts. This way you keep his rage down. A jealous man does not have any reasoning at all.

Jealousy is always a problem in a marriage. Ownership is very prevalent to a jealous person. They want you to stay where they put you, and wait until they move you from their place. Some get angry when you laugh, talk, and socialize with people.

The slave mentality is always with a jealous spirited person.

They really cannot understand true love with no shackles.

Been there and done that. Thank God I am free.

God has given me this revelation knowledge about this woman at the well. I can feel her pain dealing with jealousy I myself have been in some very jealousy situations. When you be true to yourself, I have to admit only Jesus rescued me.

2. The next personality is promises.

They are always promising what they do not have, and what they are going to do. Most of the time, nothing materializes. The only true promise is JESUS CHRIST when we are so in love, we cannot see the darkness of promises. Man cannot promise us anything because he does not own anything. It all belongs to God.

But because of his good looks and the cologne he is wearing our senses are open to the flesh sensualities. The fire in our flesh can get so hot that you do not care about the promises, all you want is satisfaction.

I can imagine the woman at the well dealing with this situation, and not having any help at all. Because the men in her time treated the women like dogs. Yet with all her trauma, she came out stronger

3. The married man syndrome

How many times were we captured by somebody else husband. Listening to their lies, about their wives not cleaning their home or cooking for the family. But yet they can wine and dine you so that his evening would end up in your bed. Feeling that you owe him for such a good time, we fall for the trap. Feeling so empty inside knowing he had to leave to go back home by a certain time we still take what he has to give. Then when he leaves we beat our self down. Now we are really trapped because we want him to leave his wife to marry us. Open your eyes and see how sin can take down the road you do not want to go. The flesh is never satisfied. Life has a lot of curves. We have to be ready for how the curves come. Now, this is in modern times. Think about the time the woman at the well was living in. those times were really bad.

Only Jesus could be her answer as he is our answer to our problems. Yes, women, we pay for being naïve to the married man syndrome we get to lock into their lies, especially on holidays waiting for a phone call. Or a knock at the door. While they are home enjoying their family. You start talking to yourself, hoping that you are not being a fool about somebody else husband. Making sure you go where no one would see you being out on the town.

Wondering about how his wife really treats him. You know something is wrong but just cannot put your finger on it.

The trap is so compact that you cannot get out of the relationship like you want to. Now, what do I do in this case? Start looking for a well to meet Jesus. Jesus is the only one that will tell us the whole truth about life. In this kind of relationship, with our hearts hurting for relief. We do need Jesus to heal us with his living water and his living bread.

Notice their stories are always about their wife and what she is not doing. But yet he wants to leave the situation. We cannot let them take a toy out of us. They are always looking for a plaything. The married syndrome is very serious. Why not married Jesus. He will take care of us. The bottom line is the wife is suffering just like we are. Lies can lock us all up for a period of time. Just remember what goes around comes back around.

4. Lazy syndrome

Looking for a woman to take care of them the sad thing he does not want to work for anybody. We women out working while they are staying home running up the electric bill, eating up all our children's food.

Yes sometimes the children call him Uncle Jim. But when they get older they see us as we really were then. They have the knowledge to know what really was going on.

And we wonder why our children treat us like they do. When we look back at our situation we need a well, so we can talk to Jesus. Not only to give me a drink but to save me from myself. We hold on to the lazy man for his sex, knowing we need him to work and to help pay bills. Being crippled from the flesh with no power to operate from within. We become a slave to laziness. He will go out and stay all day, and come home with no job. Wake up sister look at the truth. He is too lazy to work.

Bills are getting out of hand. And we are so upset on the inside. All he wants to do is have sex. He is more rested than we are. Stay at the well until Jesus fills you up and give you the power to walk away from this kind of relationship.

Down the street you hear about your neighbor's daughter is pregnant by your lazy man. All you can do is cry from the pain because you do not want to kill him. Laziness is a sin. Only Jesus can work these traumas out in our life. Run to the well, quickly

RICH MAN PERSONALITY 5

Some men always give the impression of being rich. Half the time we women are caught up in a web from financial struggles, hoping to meet someone who can give us a helping hand.

But deep down in our hearts, we would like them to pay for everything. What a relief it is to know that this man will take care of me. It is a relief, but it is not always the truth. The rich man is harder to deal with because he is counting his money all the time.

The thrill is that you met a man with some money. Your smile gets bigger, you start feeling like you can relax now. What a blow to your mind when you look at all the hell you have come through to meet a solid man of wealth.

Then you find out this is just a cover to put himself in your home. Once he moves in the hell comes out at you. He has more debt than you have. He is looking for the same thing you are looking for security. Having to care for this man is a strain to your conscience.

Especially when you thought you had helped to get you out of the mess with your bills. The way he looks when he gets dressed up. His cologne was always in your nostrils, and he talks so sweetly. Caught in the rich man trap.

The woman at the well had some weight on her mind. No telephone back then, she could not call anyone to talk about her situation. Could you have survived this kind of lifestyle in her time?

So stunning in her lifestyle with this so-called rich man, she had a purpose in her heart he had to go. He was so demanding in her life. She could no longer afford his lifestyle.

How many of us are living in hell with a cover-up situation? Wondering when will it be over. They are more comfortable at home than you are.

Caught in a relationship of tears, and hurt, abuse with cursing words. And every now and then a fight breaks out. Sin has no limits. Trying to satisfy his wants and desires. And you hardly have anything for your self. Wake up Jesus is coming to your well.

The bible does not mention that the woman had any children. That is a blessing, the children do not have to suffer because of crazy sex in the house. Not being married brings crazy sex. Because the man will try to get all he can get before he leaves your house. The flesh has no limit to what it will do. It is easy to turn it on, but hard to turn it off. How many of us women have been caught in the same boat of hurts and tears, trying to take care of a man that has a bottomless bottom to his wants. The more you work the less you have for yourself. Cry out to Jesus I will meet you at the well.

The sixth man

The sixth man was the one who was just living with her for all he could get from her. Being married five times is a lot to deal with. Be careful how you let a man deal you a low blow. The main responsibility is to get an education so he can find a good job, so he can prepare for his family. Gen. 3:16-19

I believe she was so exhausted until she just gave in to the relationship. She knew she had to draw water the next day. Praying in her heart lord help me to do better. She was on her way to the well.

The seventh man

Thank God for the seventh man in her life who was Jesus. The only one who can look into our hearts. He knows who we are he shines his light down into our spirit and searches us with his light. When he sees the darkness in our heart The Holy Spirit brings it to our conscience so we can confess our sins. Jesus loved us out of hell. His love transcends all of what nature consists of His love is clean and sweet, with an everlasting promise, that he will never leave us are forsake us. That is love. His promises are sure and pure, he will never let you down. The well is the place to meet Jesus. Our lives are so dry, and messed up from all the failures and hurt until we need to be at the well so we can fill up with his living waters. For from the waters he lifted me so safe am I.

10

Sanctified woman

When she went to the well at her odd hour to avoid the other women at the well. She had no idea that Jesus was sitting on the well to give her a drink of his living water. Jesus came all the way to Samaria just to dress her situation. Look at Jesus so kind and compassionate with the woman at the well. Not only did he knew her inside and out, he dealt with every aspect of her being. He said to her to give me a drink. Being shock that he spoke to her because he was a Jew. Knowing they did not have any dealings with the Samaritans. Jesus knew she was being shy because he was a stranger to her. He said if thou knewest the gift of God. And who it is that saith to thee, Give me to drink: thou wouldest have given thee living water.

Never a man spoke to her like this. She was interested in what else he had to say. But she had nothing to draw with. She said unto him, Sir, thou hast nothing to draw with, and the well is very deep: from whence then hast thou that living water?

Art thou greater than our father Jacob, which gave us the well, and drank thereof himself, and his children, and cattle?

The conversation was getting to her heart. Jesus answered and said unto her, Who so ever drinketh of this water shall thirst again. But whosoever drinketh of the water that I shall give him shall never thirst: but the water that I shall give him shall be in him a well of water springing up, into everlasting life.

She was so excited with his conversation until she steps out on faith. The woman saith unto him, Sir, give me this water, that I thirst not, neither come here hither to draw.

The thought in her mind, that she would be free from this crowd that did not like her. I feel her excitement thinking I will be free now.

Jesus asked her to go call thy husband, and come hither.

She was truthful and honest. The woman answered and said, I have no husband. Jesus said unto her, thou hast well said, I have no husband: For thou hast had five husband; and he whom thou now hast is not thou thy husband: in that said thou truly.

The woman saith unto him, Sir. I perceived that thou are a prophet, our fathers worshipped in this mountain; and ye say, that in Jerusalem is the place where men ought to worship. Now if you notice the woman recognized that Jesus saw into her innermost soul. Now, remember that Jesus is the living word. The word is life, she could see the word, and talk to the word. What a blessing, to our soul when we think about the woman at the well talking to the true and living God this woman was so shocked by Jesus her spirit had come alive in her soul. Just one touch from Jesus will change our life. The more Jesus talks to her the more she was getting free.

She did not care what people thought about her. She had met Jesus who was a well sitting on a well waiting on her. This day she would be free from all her ills. What a blessing in her life.

Think about this Jesus a divine well sitting on an earthen well with the appearance of stone and dirt. Jesus will deliver you from your sin-sick conditions.

Now we have the written the word which is the Holy Bible,

> For the word is quick, and powerful, and sharper than any two-edged sword, piercing even to the dividing asunder of soul and spirit, and of the joints and marrow, and is a discerner of the thoughts and intents of the heart.
>
> Heb. 4:12

Jesus spoke with love and cares to the Samaritan woman. All we need someone to speak kindly to us. Kindness melts our hearts. Until she met her creator who knew her from inside out, he dealt with all of her issues at the well. He was getting her ready to evangelize for the kingdom. The truth will always set you free. Jesus is the truth.

v.13 Neither is there any creature that is not manifest in his sight: But all things are naked and opened unto the eyes of him with whom we have to do All things are naked before the Lord. So we cannot hide anything.

Just like Jesus saw the woman, at the well He also sees us His word is still working in our life, as long as we read the word of God. By this being the written word it transformed itself in our spirit and then it becomes spirit food for our life. It becomes living water that we can drink from, and within our hearts, we become filled with Jesus.

Chp.10

Let us give Jesus the Glory for who he is.1st Samuel 2:30b those who honor me I will honor.

Let us do all for the glory of God. [1cor. 10:31] we have to learn to glorify God in our bodies. [1cor.6:20]

> Even every one that is called by my name: for I created him for my glory, I have formed him; yea, I have made him.
>
> Isa. 43:7

Knowing this according to God's word we are to be totally for God's purpose. That in everything God may be glorified through Jesus Christ. And Jesus lives in us so we belong to the master. Thank God for his living water, and his keeping power.

Jesus is the best lover in town. We must suffer through some things, but God will lift you up through his word. Remember Jesus cried with a loud voice If any man thirst let him come unto me and drink. Drink from the fountain of living waters. A fountain that will never run dry.

Come with joy so you can draw water out of the well of Jesus. He is the well of salvation. This living water is eternal. Call upon His name and declare him as Lord in your life. Declare his doings among the people, that his name will be exalted. Sing unto the lord, for he hath done excellent things.

Have you been delivered from the hell of sin, and wash in his blood? Think about it over and over again. Jesus is the living water. Jesus has living water. His well is deep enough for all to get a drink of this life-changing water. Praise him for who he is.

What the woman at the well did not know, that Jesus was preparing her to evangelize the whole city. We must be equipped to do God's will. We have to study to show our selves approved unto God. Because being a workman in the field, we cannot be or feel ashamed. When you have studied the word, you will walk in boldness.

> Having, therefore, brethren boldness to enter into the holiest by the blood of Jesus.
>
> Hebrews 10:19

We must have the boldness to stand in the power of his might. Look at

> For it is God which worketh in you both to will and to do of his good pleasure. Every good work we do is to his good pleasure.
>
> Phil. 2:13

v.13 says [Do all things without murmurings and disputing's. We complain too much about nothing. We keep the enemy happy when we complain. The enemy will keep us from coming together through gossip, lies, unrest, clicks, hatred, the big I, and every sin that so easily upset us. Let Jesus work a work in you. He is working a work in me even as I write this book. And I am glad. Because I want to go deeper in the LORD.

Jesus worked work with the woman at the well. There is nothing too hard for God. In order to minister for the lord, we must have the boldness of the Holy Ghost. Not only that we must be contagious in love. God's love goes all the way to the Spirit and the Soul.

Remember that the word of God is quick, powerful, and sharper than any two-edged sword, piercing even to the dividing asunder of soul and spirit, and of the joints and marrow, and is a discerner of thoughts and intents of the heart.

What is the intent of your heart right now? Which way are your thoughts flowing?

Heb. 4:12

So we can now see how important it is to tell what the Bible says about God's word. Hearing Jesus speak to her about living water brought about a change in her heart. She had the living word piercing her very being. Courage rose up in her mind. Boldness was caught her tongue, so she could be ready to run and tell somebody about Jesus.

When you are filled with this living water, there is a power of boldness that takes over in your spirit. Yes, it makes you want to run and tell somebody about Jesus.

Especially when all the trash and hidden secrets have been a washout of your heart. And you are filled with Jesus, his word, and the Holy Spirit. God is love. His love must be possessed your heart and mind. You will have the power of the [I can't help it.] With fire, burning down, in your spirit. You have to tell somebody.

Look at the woman at the well, look at what she said in the 25th verse. "The woman saith unto him, I know that Messiah cometh, which is called Christ: when he comes, he will tell us all things. Christ is his anointed name.

Jesus saith unto her, I that speak unto thee am he. When you know that you are in the divine presence of God, you really cannot explain it. She was anointed, appointed, filled, and sent to do her witnessing.

The woman at the good talk to Jesus himself, she left her water pot, and went her way into the city, and saith unto the men, come; see a man, which told me all things that ever I did: is not this the Christ. She was so bold and contagious with the living water she starts evangelizing the whole city. She did not worry about the peoples anymore. She was on fire for the master. Everything changes when you meet Jesus. And that is what we need is some living water from Jesus.

We, women, and need someone who will love us unconditionally no matter what our circumstances are Jesus knows who we are, He understands our hurts and bruises in life that we encounter. He knows all about our inner man thirst, the depths of our secret wounds, our wants, and all our needs.

When we think about how we have been treated in our marriage. The way our husband ran around with other women while we were trying to be the best we could be, keeping the house clean, taking care of the children, just doing all a wife knows how to do. To think that was not good enough for him. Yet we ask ourselves what did she have that we did not have? Did she look better than we did or was that the real dog in our husband to run on us?

Let us take it to Jesus. Only he knows. He knows just how much we can bear.

What a mighty God we serve. Only He and He alone know how to satisfy us. Because He made us, He created us with all these sensitive areas He is the Author and finisher of our faith.

> And ye are complete in him, which is the head of all principalities and power.
>
> Colossians 2:10

Jesus knew women would need him completely to handle all our secret fires those are burning down in our heart. We have to stop holding things in our minds and in our hearts. Just turn it all over to Jesus, he will work them out. There is no matter what he cannot solve. No fire that he cannot put out. No dryness he cannot water, and no cold place he cannot heat up. Turn all over to Jesus, he will meet you in at your well.

Sometime when you are laying down talk to him, he is listening to your deepest cry. Just one drink will enlighten your eyes so you can see the harvest of souls that has to be won for the kingdom.

> Seek ye the LORD while he may be found, call ye upon him while he is near. ⁷Let the wicked forsake his way, and the unrighteous man his thoughts: and let him return unto the LORD, and he will have mercy upon him; and to our God, for he will abundantly pardon. ⁸For my thoughts are not your thoughts, neither are your ways my ways, saith the LORD.
>
> Isa.55:6-8

We all have strayed away at certain times. Let us return back to the well so we can be refreshed by Jesus with his living water life can leave you dry. Problems have no respect for a person. You have to encourage yourself. You cannot rely on your shape body thinking that you got what it takes. Our bodies are changing every day. As you get older things starts to sage. Jesus is the only one we can depend on. He is the only one who will be there in the good times and the bad times. Your flesh will fail you. You cannot hold to know the man with your flesh. In the midst of your pains and doubt cry out now. When you are tired of being tired cry out to Jesus he will see you through. Women wake up! Jesus is the man of the hour. The man of power, the man of joy, the man of peace, the man of everlasting love.

He owns the universe, He is the pattern of the universe, He is the pattern of the tabernacle, He gave us his righteousness, so we can talk to God the Father at any time.

> ᵇHe became our sacrificial lamb. And washed us from our sins in his own blood. And hath made us kings and priests unto God and his Father; to him be glory and dominion forever and ever A—men
>
> Rev. 1:5b,6

Our conscience has to be purged from dead works so we can serve the true and living God. [Hebrews 9:14]

We cannot serve God until we are willing to trust the blood to purge our conscience from dead works. The past cannot go where the future is. Jesus paid for us with his own blood. He was willing to die on the cross so he could have a big spiritual family. One day we will be around the throne with God the Father, God the Son, and God the Holy Spirit.

Even though we were so mess up in sin, look at this verse in how it explains the way God saw us.

> Where in time past ye walked according to the course of this world, according to the prince of the power of the air, the spirit that now worketh in the children of disobedience.
>
> Eph. 2:2

You see the Bible is true. this verse shows us that nobody is perfect.

> Everyone has sinned and come short of the glory of God.
>
> Romans 3:23

This is why I love this story because it shows Jesus' love for mankind. There is no problem he cannot solve. All we have to do is take it to Jesus. The spirit of disobedience is still around. We want it our way. Our way has caused us pain, death and hurt. Remember God works all things after the counsel of his own will. Everything runs and is callout according to the counsel of his own will.

Jesus died for the sins of the whole world. He is calling us from every walk of life. There is no sin so great that we cannot be saved from, except the sin against the Holy Ghost.

The devil does not care who he uses. He is looking for victims. The tattoo god has taken over a lot of bodies, and minds. If you get one he will encourage you to get another one. The spirit of disobedience is subtle in all its ways. Leviticus 19:28. Matter of fact read the 19: 20 of Leviticus. What is going on now is nothing new under the Sun.

God had a purpose for the woman at the well. HIS purpose was an Eternal purpose. [Eph. 3:11] According to the eternal purpose which he purposed in Christ Jesus our Lord. His purpose gave her boldness and access with confidence by the faith of him. That she was able to run and witness in the power of his might. God does not have coward soldiers. We must stand in his resurrected power as bold soldiers reporting for duty. God's eternal purpose is to his glory. He gets all the praise. We must walk worthy of the vocation wherewith you are called.

Do you know what you are called to do? We are called to praise Him. We are called to be holy without blame before him in love. Jesus made us Holy by giving us His Holy Divine Nature. In other words, we have His DNA. This is why we can walk like Jesus, we imitators of Christ. We walk worthy of the vocation that He has called us to. That is to walk in love. We are called into the adoption by Jesus Christ to himself, according to the good pleasure of his will. We are called to his good pleasure which he hath purposed in himself. That we should be to the praise of his glory, who first trusted in Christ. We are called to be Holy, set apart for his use. Sanctified filled with his Spirit. Because we are accepted in the beloved.

Remember He has chosen us in him before the foundation of the world, that we should be holy and without blame before him in love. [Eph. 1:4]

The woman at the well needed a transformation in her inner man. When she drank the living water that Jesus gave her, she could see her eternal purpose was to be a living witness for Jesus.

Your inner man must be built up in prayer and in the word.

> We have to ask God the Father of glory to give us the Spirit of wisdom and revelation in the knowledge of him. We need our eyes of understanding being enlightened; that ye may know what the hope of his calling is, and what the riches of the glory of his inheritance in the saints.
>
> Eph.1:17,18

The woman at the well had Jesus all to herself. She did not have to read and study as we do. She got it all at one time. Just one drink of the living water brought about a change in her being. An eternal change. How would you have handle talking to Jesus in the flesh? Just think about it. We are closer than that. He is living inside of us every moment of our lives. The Holy Spirit will guide us into all truth. The truth is we need Jesus.

We are conformed into His image every day. From glory to glory, and faith, to faith. We are in the now faith realm. We need his faith to work in us. Because his faith is holy. Our natural faith is contaminated. Everything we get from Jesus is holy. Our joy is holy, our peace is holy. All our spiritual being from the inside of our heart, mind soul and spirit is holy. Whatever the blood touches it becomes holy. We need to see ourselves holy like God the Father sees us through his Son blood. God the Father is Holy He cannot look at sin. Only through the blood of Jesus does he see us as his children. We must be born again. We are not just going to heaven in just any kind of way. We have to be born of the Spirit and washed with his blood. Jesus is the door to heaven. Read the 10th chapter of St. John. And we are his Sheep. Praise the Lord for the green pastures he has for us to go in and out of. We women must keep our minds focus on our dreams and passion. There are so many gifts and talents the Lord has given us to use for his glory. We do not have to wish for what others have. We do not have to show our bodies to the world for attention. Jesus will accept us as we are. [Thank you, Jesus.] We all have a set time and season to be blessed. But meanwhile, let us study our Bible and learn of Him.

Sometimes we get so caught up in the fashion of the world until we lose our way toward our destiny. Yes, we even get stuck in a rut of trying to make a good decision for our life. When Jesus who is our life has made a way already for us to follow daily. He shines his light in us through the person of the Holy Spirit. Where he leads me I will follow. When we become real with ourselves, and get our focus on Jesus, then we can really drink from the well of peace and joy.

The woman at the well was so full of the living water that Jesus gave her, his eternal purpose came alive in her being. She had to run and tell somebody, that she found a man. A real man that could satisfy her totally. What a man, what a man, the woman at the well was so happy that she left the water pot, her old identity. Ladies we have to leave the old things behind. We have to keep reaching, keep pushing; Jesus will meet you at the well.

The change will come when Jesus moves into our hearts. Yes, it is a heart situation. Not the clothes we wear, nor the car we drive. Yet we do need them. It is about a new heart, new mind, new joy, and new peace. When we can go tell somebody I am sorry for the way I mistreated you. Learning how to humbly our selves under the mighty hand of God. In due time He will exalt you. Let God arise and His enemies are scattered. God has no respect of person. He loves us even when we do not love ourselves. What a mighty God we serve.

Today is the day of Salvation; you can accept Jesus today, Recognize that you are a sinner and you need to save. Repent. Just say from your heart lord save me from my sins. I accept Jesus as my personal Saviour. I receive the blood to purge my conscience from all dead works. Thank you for saving me now you are in the family of God.

There are 56 things that happen when you get saved.

- You are the elect of God [Rom.8:29]
- You are predestinated [Eph.1:11]
- You are chosen [1peter 2:4]
- You are called [1Thess.5:24]
- Reconciled [by God] Col.1:20
- Redeemed [Col.1:14]
- Sins covered by Atoning Blood[1Peter 2:24]
- Crucified with Christ [Gal.2:20]
- Buried with Christ. [Col.2:12]
- Adopted [Rom. 8:15]
- Forgiven all trespasses [Col. 1:14]

Thank God for a new life. Start reading your Bible. Start reading the book of St. John. Get into a Bible teaching Church. You will have new friends that love s to talks about Jesus. Start thanking God for Jesus. You will find that your heart will be filled with joy. The new life is a step by step living. Ladies look to the hills for this is where your help comes from. You do not have to live in an abusive situation. Get help before you be killed. The devil who is the prince of the power of the air is trying to destroy all of God's people. Thank God we have His word, His Blood, The Holy Spirit to protect us from the wiles of the enemy. Glory to God.

> Even when we were dead [slain] by [our own] shortcomings and trespasses, He made us alive together in fellowship and in union with Christ; He gave us the very life of Christ Himself, the same new life with He quickened Him. For it is by grace [His favor and mercy which you did not deserve] that you are saved [delivered from judgment and made partakers of Christ's salvation.
>
> Ephesians 2:5 [Amplified Bible]

I ask these questions are you the woman at the well today?